EMPLOYEE RETENTION
FUNDAMENTALS

No Nonsense Strategies To Retain Your **Best People**

Jeff Kortes

ISBN: 978-0-988307-001

Book Design by Andrew Welyczko

Contents

Introduction

Put Yourself in a Position To Win

THERE ISN'T AN organization anywhere that doesn't have a problem *of some type* with turnover. If you think that's not true, you are probably losing a ton of money. Your turnover may be relatively low... but is it still costing you money, hurting customer satisfaction, lowering quality, or perhaps resulting in the loss of that occasional top performer who really impacts your organization? IF you work the tips in each section as you read the book and begin taking ACTION on other ideas you think of as you read this book, you will get RESULTS. The ideas in this book have worked for me and I have seen them work in other organizations.

I'm not a believer in setting some target number. Why? Because then the number becomes the goal and you will start to make excuses if you don't hit the number... or worse yet... start manipulating your data to justify not hitting your number. In some cases, I have seen people hang on to a lousy employee because they are paranoid that someone will get on them about their retention number. In some cases, as you will see later, it is to your benefit to get rid of a lousy employee. What I do advocate is that you begin working on the activities, develop a strategy after a short period of time and EXECUTE on that strategy. The results will follow... I guarantee it!

As you start trying the activities listed in every chapter, you will see your retention strategy begin to develop. Performing the activities is like building a block tower just like the ones we all built as kids. We built it one block at a time and no two towers ever looked alike. How sturdy the tower is depends on you. The shape of the tower is up to you as well. When I present my "No Nonsense Retention" speech, I tell the participants that their goal is to develop their own tower. Make the tower your own.

How hard you work at your retention tower or who else in your organization you get involved will be up to you. The first step is that you got the book. The second is that you have started to read it. If once you start to read you begin to try the **TIPS,** you are on your way to developing a successful retention strategy for your department, division, company or entity for which you are responsible. At the risk of sounding self-serving, you will know if you are serious if—once you have finished reading this book and decide you are committed to policies like these—you go to the boss and tell him "We need one of these books for all our supervisors and managers!" Why? Because then you have started to put your money where your mouth is.

Art by Nick Aringer

Once you start to ante up some cash, you will want to see the fruits of your labor and the momentum of multiple leaders in the organization working the process together.

As you start to work on the **TIPS** or other ideas you see you will see a strategy start to emerge... and you WILL start to see some success... which will get you hungry for more. I don't advocate that you read everything and then try to develop some grand plan. Just start trying the **TIPS**. That's the beginning of building your retention tower. What you are doing is no different from what famous athletes do. In *From Grunt to Greatness* (Business Growth Solutions, 2005) Tiger Woods talks about "putting himself in a position to win on the back nine on Sunday." He knows that a tournament is 72 holes. His goal is built over the course of the previous 63 holes... shot by shot. Your retention tower is built block by block. Systematically!

About the Author

Jeff Kortes has more than 30 years of experience in the human resources field. He has worked at companies that specialize in heavy manufacturing, construction, textiles and software development. During Jeff's entire career, he has worked to attract, retain and energize employees, at all levels, at companies including ConAgra Foods, Midas International, Quaker Oats, global manufacturing, industrial equipment supplier SPX, cookware maker Regal Ware Worldwide, and sock maker Wigwam Mills, Inc. He has helped businesses with as few as ten employees compete with larger employers in attracting and retaining the talent they needed to survive and thrive.

Jeff has experienced the pressure of retaining good people in booming economies and has personally fought the "retention wars," while seeking intellectual talent—in software development, among production workers at a hosiery mill, and among skilled trades at manufacturing plants and at construction sites.

Jeff has always taken a "no nonsense" approach to Human Resources that is based on common sense and sound, basic approaches to dealing with people. His decision to write this book was driven by his disappointment that no one had written a book that applied these basic principles in a way that was easy to understand and apply. He observed that organizations often got too "fancy" and lost sight of the basics. And if the basics were done well, companies produced excellent retention results, even in the most competitive marketplaces. That philosophy is at the heart of this book.

Jeff knew his approach worked, but he also wanted to know what had worked for other Human Resources professionals and line managers. He researched those who had been the most successful and spoke with them. Armed with their thoughts as well as his own knowledge and experience, Jeff began to assemble a book that would be a "no nonsense" primer on retaining employees in any industry. This is that book.

Jeff is a member of the National Speakers Association (NSA) and a frequent speaker on the topic of retention, to Human Resources departments and associations, and business groups. Jeff also runs his own company, Human Asset Management, which helps organizations recruit, retain and develop their best people.

What's Turnover Costing You?

I HAVE SEEN countless formulas and studies designed to determine what turnover costs an organization. Everything I have seen indicates that the best measure of the cost of turnover is roughly three months of salary for every person who leaves. Another formula I have seen sets the cost of turnover for entry-level employees at 30 to 50 percent of their annual salary, for mid-level employees at 150 percent of their annual salary and, for upper-level employees, as high as 400 percent of their annual salary. A third formula I have seen determines the cost of turnover by taking 25 percent of the annual salary for every employee lost. Using any of these calculations, the numbers can be staggering if you are running at 10 percent turnover.

Some people might say these numbers are overstated. But think about what it costs a company when a middle-level manager walks out the door and a key deadline is missed or a major opportunity is not seized because no one can fill the manager's shoes. This is particularly true in knowledge-based businesses. When I worked in the computer industry, we could easily calculate our cost when software developers would leave and a product roll-out would be delayed. The numbers were mind-boggling. Imagine the impact you'd have on your bottom-line if you could cut turnover in half, to 5 percent. That cost savings is huge, even with better retention of just your lower-level employees. All of your resources walk on two feet and when those feet walk out the door, so does the knowledge they carry with them.

Once you choose a number as a target or a formula you will use to calculate the cost of turnover, stick with it. Don't start adjusting your measures to feel better about where you are going, because the good feeling will vanish when your profits start to deteriorate. Your good people will likely jump ship when they will realize you aren't addressing the problem and that you are in denial. *Once turnover starts to accelerate, it is very hard to slow down, much less stop.*

I recommend that you start classifying each instance of turnover as "good," "bad" or "neutral" turnover. Some turnover is good. Yes, that's what I said! There are times when you have to fire people or permanently reduce your workforce. That's reality. If you want to take that into account when calculating your turnover, by all means do so. (Just don't play games with the numbers to make yourself feel better about your lousy turnover. Again, whatever method you chose, use the same measurement over time.) When you fire a non-performer, it should fall into the good turnover category. When a top performer leaves to go to elsewhere, it's bad turnover. Neutral turnover would include employees who retire.

Classify your turnover. Then track the three types of employees you are losing. This will force your managers to determine the quality of the people who are leaving. It will also force them to discuss the turnover with HR, whether it's good, bad or neutral. That dialog will enable upper management to evaluate how realistic different managers are. It will also reveal which managers are just making excuses for their own failings at taking the steps necessary to retain top people. Trends will become very evident in various operating units, plants or departments. If you are a plant manager, general manager, VP or owner, you will want to monitor your turnover numbers and ask questions about what activities are taking place to reduce it.

From this point forward, you need to adopt a no-excuses mentality when it comes to bad turnover. You will look closely at your bad turnover and realize it is turnover that is not acceptable. And then you will take action to address it. No Excuses!

no nonsense notes

▶ Everyone's approach to retention is different. Decide what your strategy will be.

▶ Determine how you will calculate the cost of turnover... then stick with the calculation you chose to measure all future performance.

▶ Not all turnover is bad! Classify turnover as "good," "bad" or "neutral," and track it.

▶ Adopt a no-excuses mentality regarding bad turnover.

The Supervisory Difference

SEVENTY-FIVE PERCENT OF people say the worst thing about their job is their boss. That is a stinging indictment of management today. I have always contended that most people do not retire because they want to. They retire because they get tired of all the "nonsense" they have to go through at work. Most of the nonsense is usually a result of the way their boss treats them. If you read no further than this section, retention in your organization will improve because *your supervisory and management team is the engine that drives retention. Their boss* is the most important person in any strategy you employ to retain your best people.

The role of the boss is built into every section of this book because the boss and his or her actions are *everything* when it comes to retention. A company that has great leadership will have great retention, and happy, satisfied and engaged employees. And, let's face it, the vast majority of bosses are not directors, VPs or presidents. They are supervisors, team leaders, department managers, plant managers and so on. The power and success of an organization is driven by these people more than anyone... even if the VPs and presidents think it's driven by them. When Marcus Buckingham and Curt Coffman conducted studies for their book *First, Break All the Rules* (Simon & Schuster, 1999), they found that high-performing organizations were a function of the managers...not the senior executives.

If you supervise people *at any level*, you need to take a good, close look at yourself in the mirror. If you're senior management, you need to take a look at the leaders in your organization as well as yourself. Leaders need to possess the skills and value systems required to sustain an organization into the next generation because—to 90 percent of your people—THE SUPERVISORS ARE THE COMPANY! They are the horses you will ride to the finish line. How well you do as an organization depends on the quality of this group.

First, look at their value system. If they are the type of leaders who do not treat people with respect, who make excuses when things go wrong, who say one thing and do another, who complain about things they are asked to do, who have turnover in their department or who show other signs that they are not solid leaders, it's time to act. (For more on the characteristics you should be looking for, *First, Break All the Rules* is a great resource.)

You probably can't do much about someone who has a lousy value system. If they have a lousy value system, get rid of them. This is not an excuse for you to wipe out those supervisors who don't always agree with you. It's a call to action to address any supervisors whose value system does not include the view that people add value to a company. In most cases, you can train their brains out and nothing will change. Figure out where that might be the case and take action. Either move such supervisors into non-leadership roles or remove them from the organization. Then, replace them with people who know how to lead. Retention in their area will increase immediately.

Unfortunately, identifying and removing poor managers is not that easy. In some cases—and this is where it gets tricky—supervisors simply do not have the skills to lead. The answer? Give them the skills. Basic supervisory training is one of the most overlooked areas in organizations. Don't believe me? Look at how quickly training budgets are cut when things get tough. Did I just describe your organization? You need to assess how various supervisors manage their people. Those who do not delegate, who can't make decisions, who micro-manage and who fail to hold their people accountable will bury your organizations, but, in many cases, they may have fallen into a rut and simply need to be reminded of their role in order to get back on track.

The number of large organizations that do not provide uniform, basic leadership skills training on an ongoing basis is astonishing. The key is uniform, basic and consistent training over time. If your leadership training does not meet those three criteria, you are missing the boat and losing money because of it. Uniform, basic and consistent training over time is important when it comes to reinforcing the organization's value system and developing skills.

My clients tend to be privately-run businesses or stand-alone units that are growing. Why? They are usually led

TIP

When was the last time you or your organization did basic supervisory skills training (if ever)? If it has been more than three years, schedule a refresher course for everyone. If training has never occurred, call me... or someone like me... to get you that training. Sending your supervisors and managers out to work with your people without giving them any fresh basic skills is like sending an army to fight a war with outdated weapons. The result: You are going to lose the war!

by someone who has a vested interest in the success of the business, someone who knows that their supervisors are the key to their success. So they invest the money because they know they will get a payback. They are not worried about spending a few bucks on training. Maybe that's why they are growing and profitable!

What can *you* do if you're a manager and your organization has chosen not to implement a leadership training series? Talk to Human Resources. If they give you an excuse about why it's not happening, find training on your own and ask if they will pay for it. If they say no, pay for it yourself and do it on your own! Invest in yourself. It's your career, not the company's, and when your job is eliminated, the facility closes or something

TIP

Take 30 minutes to sit down in a quiet room and think about your two worst supervisors or managers. Write down their names. Then ask yourself: Do they have the values your organization needs? If not, then develop a plan to change that or to remove them from the organization. This may not be the total answer to your supervisory problem, but it is a huge step in the right direction!

else happens to force you to look for work elsewhere, you are prepared. If you remain there, you will use those skills to be more successful than your peers who sat back and coasted.

I heard this quote over 25 years ago. It stuck in my mind and has influenced my work philosophy. Let's talk about how it should impact your actions as a leader. If you bought this book, you are clearly look-

> **"I'm not trying to clean up the world, only my little corner"**
>
> Hawkeye Pierce,
> *M*A*S*H*

ing for a way to lead that improves retention. Leadership really comes down to *you*, regardless of what the choices your organization makes. You can lead in your own department or area. I like the term "sphere of influence" to describe the place where you can have an impact. I have worked with corporations that were employee-relations nightmares within which one plant, neverthe-less, proved a shining example of how to lead. How? Because the plant manager chose to lead differently and all of his people followed his lead. His leadership style was his own, and, despite the overall philosophy of the parent company, his style of leadership revolved primar-ily around employee relations.

The same is true whether it's your team or depart-ment. Like Hawkeye Pierce, you need to concentrate on cleaning up your area of responsibility. You will drive yourself crazy if you try to solve all of the location or facility's problems, much less those of the rest of the organization. Concentrate on your sphere of influence, regardless of its size, and create your own little island within the organization by controlling what you can control... which is *a lot*. What can you control? You can certainly control the following:

▶ Your attitude (develop a "YES! Attitude")
▶ How well you communicate.
▶ How you treat people (it should be with respect...
   always!)
▶ Whether you set a positive example.
▶ How much you care for your people.
▶ How genuine you are.

How you treat your people has more to do with turnover than any other factor. You have seen it yourself in organizations where you have worked. Certain managers tend to churn through people, even the people the managers hire themselves. No one in their departments is happy. They are running the corporate version of a jail and people are doing time because they have to and will get out as they can. Compare that to those managers who tend to be people magnets. Everyone wants to work for them! Their people will go the extra mile for them. When you are in their areas, you can feel the positive energy.

Look at the lousy ones. Here is what you will observe:

▶ They micro-manage their people and will not
   delegate.
▶ They send mixed messages about what they want.
▶ They blame their people for lack of performance or
   complain that they can't trust the people in their
   department to get the job done.
▶ Nothing is ever good enough for them.
▶ They take credit for the successes of their people.

The end result? Their departments have a revolving door. When asked why their turnover is so high, they will use such excuses as, "I demand more from my people than other managers," or "You just can't find good peo-ple," or "People have no work ethic," and on and on. You know who those managers are in your organization. This type of manager will not survive into the next decade because retention is expected to be the biggest chal-lenge organizations will face. Due to the predicted short-age of good people to fill necessary jobs, organizational survival will depend upon companies keeping turnover low. As a result, the behavior of these managers will not be tolerated.

Your goal: DON'T BE ONE OF THEM! If you started to get uncomfortable reading the excuses or behaviors listed here, you need to do a gut check and ask yourself if you are one of "those" managers. If you are... change... or get out of management, because you are a major cause of turnover in your organization.

Do it for yourself. Stop complaining and lead. It's as simple as that. Your people will love you. You will be happier. Try each **TIP** as you read on. You will be much happier in your role because you will see the difference... and so will your people.

> Conduct a personal gut check right now! Re-read the items on the previous page and check off all of the ones that apply to you. Be honest with yourself. Then look at the items you checked and start working on changing yourself. Start today.
>
> **TIP**

In the end, how you are viewed is a function of your credibility and the trust your people have in you. If you have these things going for you, you are going to be a retention magnet. All of the actions and traits discussed in this section in particular and in this book overall are designed to build your credibility and the trust your people will have in you. If you possess credibility, people will trust you. If they trust you, they are far less likely to quit. It's that simple.

Don't complain the next time something doesn't go well. Instead, when you talk to your people, substitute the following words for anything you would normally say: "We will find a way to solve this problem." Then watch how differently your people react. You have gone from being viewed as a drain on the attitudes of everyone in the organization to being a person who leads by example. Your people will feel better about you... and you will feel a lot better about yourself.

- 75 percent of the people in this country feel the worst thing about their job is their boss. Resolve to be in the other 25 percent.

- Provide uniform, basic leadership training for your management team on an ongoing basis.

- Invest in your own training if the company won't invest in you.

- Take ownership of your "sphere of influence" and resolve to make things better in that sphere.

- Control what you can control... and that is quite a bit!

- Stop complaining, blaming others and whining. Instead, start to lead.

Visibility: Management By Walking Around

THIS CONCEPT IS the Holy Grail of retention. It is the Holy Grail of management. Tom Peters captured it when he wrote *In Search of Excellence* twenty years ago. The executives at Xerox got it when they designed a training program so managers would get out of their offices, over thirty years ago. Visibility is timeless. Yet we tend to return to the caves we call our offices and hibernate. We cut ourselves off from our people and the very information we need to run our businesses. We also cut out one of the most effective retention tools at our disposal: visibility.

Early in my career as an employee relations supervisor (yes, it was about our relationship with our employees "back in the day," as my son would say), I worked with a general manager we'll call Rob. Rob assumed responsibility for a facility that was in major trouble. Productivity was terrible, delivery times were abysmal and morale was so low nobody wanted to come to work.

The first thing Rob did was take a morning "stroll" through the facility, something he did every morning and afternoon from then on. The facility was a sprawling operation that ran 24/7 with rotating shifts. It was incredibly hard to communicate with employees, much less see them in person. Not for Rob. Rob went out every morning and every afternoon like clockwork. At 7:30 a.m., he'd "stroll" around the facility and chat with the third shift as they were leaving and with the first shift as they were arriving in the morning. Then at 2:30 p.m. Rob would catch the first shift as they were ending their day and the second shift who were coming on. People loved talking with Rob and he knew everyone. He also knew everything that was going on at the facility. He was able to use that information to make operational decisions that drove success. In a matter of months, productivity was up, delivery times were down, accident rates fell and morale was on the rise. The facility started making money and, on every shift, people were glad to come to in. Rob spent two hours a day being highly visible, so visible that people noticed when HE WASN'T AROUND! They loved it. They loved him. And... he learned more about what was going on operationally and with our people.

For some odd reason, managers in offices and white collar environments make themselves far less visible than those in manufacturing even though, ironically, it's easier to be visible to their employees since most white-collar employees work the day shift.

This is one of the most important things you will get from this book. It's simple. REAL simple. GET OUT OF YOUR OFFICE. That's the answer. If you get out of your office, walk around the facility, observe, listen to and say "hello" to people, you will have moved light years past the vast majority of your competition.

This may come as a shock to most managers, but your people actually *want* to see you, and they *like* talking to you. Walking around will make you unique in management today. Why? Because everyone sits in their offices or cubes and sends emails to their people, even if their people are two feet away... Or they text them. All of the electronic communications at our disposal give us excuses not to be visible. Consequently, it's easy to hide in the office and avoid face-to-face communication.

The very communication technology aimed at making us an information-based society is cutting us off from our people – the very people who can provide us with information! We find ourselves emailing the people in the cube next to us. That's great if we are dealing with a simplistic issue. Unfortunately, most of the issues with people are NOT simplistic. Email is not what's called a "channel rich" communication method because it eliminates the ingredients key to communication: the tone of your voice, facial expression and body language.

Email also fails to give us the opportunity to get to know who our people are, what's important to them, what they like about working in our organization, and why they stay. How many people do you know who will tell you in an email that their teenage daughter is pregnant or that their wife's cancer treatments are going well? No one that I know of. For those of you who are thinking,

"That's none of my business," I have one thing to say to you: it is your business. Those are the issues that distract people, the problems that keep people from doing their job or being engaged at work. If you can help them, you become human to them and people like to work for someone who cares. Why? Because too many bosses don't. If people don't want to talk about it, that's fine too of course. BUT IF THEY DO WANT TO TALK, you could blow a great opportunity to get to know your people and to understand what makes them tick... or to know when the watch is broken! My experience is that most people love to talk to other people about what's going on in their lives. When you talk with your people face-to-face, you also give yourself a leg up on your competition in the retention war.

Because the bulk of a person's message is conveyed via his body language and non-verbal cues, much is lost when we communicate via phone, email, texting or even written memo. This leads to miscommunication, confusion and a host of other problems. According to *Modern Management: Diversity, Quality, Ethics, and the Global Environment*, only 7 percent of your message is conveyed through your words, 35 percent through your body language and the remaining 45 percent through such non-verbal means as facial expressions and the tone of your voice. No wonder people often take emails the wrong way!

The result of hiding behind electronics is that we now have a generation of managers who do not know how to walk around, make small talk and, in many cases, are afraid to talk to people in person.

The president and owner of a company that is a client of mine walks through the office and the shop four times a day. He ALWAYS makes it a point to walk around before he leaves so he sees everyone on the second shift. This provides people with an opportunity to ask questions, bring up issues and concerns, find out how business is going and so on. It gives him an opportunity to take the pulse of the organization, to examine product quality and to communicate with the people. Here's how it works:

- ▶ Visibility provides accessibility.
- ▶ Accessibility creates an opportunity to communicate.
- ▶ Communication provides an opportunity to solve problems.
- ▶ Problem-solving builds credibility... it also helps your productivity and quality.
- ▶ Credibility builds trust.
- ▶ People like people they can trust.
- ▶ If they like you, they are far less likely to leave!
- ▶ Therefore... VISIBILITY DRIVES RETENTION!

The other operational benefits to visibility are enormous as well. As you walk around you will spot quality problems, workflow issues and customer service needs. Walking around will make you money while driving retention in the process.

The best way to ensure that you are visible is to develop a regular routine for walking around. Take a "stroll" around twice a day, at a minimum, first thing in the morning and late in the day. A walk first thing in the morning gives you an opportunity to see if there are issues that need to be addressed, to find out if your people need anything, or to pass along critical information before the workday gets into full swing. A walk late in the day enables you to plan ahead for the next day if adjustments are necessary or to convey necessary information to your people. It also gives you an opportunity to "chat" with your people in person... not online.

These strolls afford an opportunity to interact, to get to know your people. They create opportunities to communicate. People will become comfortable talking with you. As you communicate, you will soon learn what's important to your people, information that is critical to have when you conduct performance management discussions and career growth sessions. You will learn what these people are jazzed about doing—insight that is invaluable. Besides, you will actually have fun doing it! If you don't... you need to get out of management!

You will also get an opportunity to know your people as individuals. This knowledge is crucial. It will enable you to notice changes in a person's behavior. These changes may indicate that there's something wrong at work for one individual or another; these changes may even indicate that a person is thinking of leaving! If you sense such a change, a red flag should go up: Something is going wrong and you need to ask questions to determine what it is. Then take action!

Changes in behavior can also alert you to issues people are facing outside of work. These issues can also impact their ability to perform on the job. 20 percent of the people on the job at any one time are facing issues that distract them from focusing on their job. The cost to your business is staggering.

Worse yet, behavioral changes may also signal that someone is at an emotional tipping point. Forklift accidents used to be the number one cause of fatalities in the workplace. Today, the number one cause of fatalities in the workplace is violence. Your visibility may enable you to observe behaviors and to pick up on issues that are red flags for potential violent behavior. You can then take steps to head it off by working with your Human Resources department, which can intervene with professional assistance.

When I give my "No Nonsense Retention" speech, I am shocked to hear from my audiences that fewer than 5 percent of the participants get out of their offices and stroll around daily. These are a mix of department managers, human resources managers and senior level executives. What's their excuse? "I don't have the time." My response? It's your job... make the time. You are there to lead people. The best way to lead them is to talk to them, and increasing your visibility is the best way to create opportunities to talk to them.

> On your calendar, block out 30-60 minutes twice a day for an "employee meeting" and use the time to get out of your office and stroll around the cube or factory floor. You're not lying... You will be meeting with all of your people... just not in a conference room. SCHEDULE IT AND "STROLL" AROUND!

TIP

no nonsense notes

▶ Get out of your office... take a stroll... and get "face-to-face" with your people every day!

▶ Visibility drives retention.

▶ Find out what makes your people tick.

▶ 93 percent of your message is conveyed via your body language, the tone of your voice, and other non-verbal cues.

▶ At any given time, 20 percent of your workforce has personal issues that may affect their work performance.

4

Care About Your People

I DO BELIEVE that most managers truly care about people. And I believe you can care and still get the job done. Unfortunately, amidst the frenzy of work, we often forget that this is an integral part of being a good manager or supervisor. It is particularly important if you're in human resources. The pace of work, combined with the occasional unpleasant moments dealing with people tends to jade managers over time. Hopefully, you will be jolted out of that state of mind as you read this section and are reminded of the importance of caring. If you don't care for people... get out of management. It's as pure and simple as that. If you don't, you will remain miserable your entire career.

Caring is at the heart of being a *great* supervisor, human resources professional or executive. People know if you care... and they know if you don't. People have an innate instinct about this and they can tell. It's something you just can't fake. Assuming you have the capacity to care, the key is learning how to show you care to your people. People are far less likely to quit if they know you care about them. The decision to leave is no longer simply business. It becomes personal. More often than not, people quit because of a boss. They are far less likely to quit a *caring* boss.

Know Your People

Know your people. This is crucial to being a caring boss. Where did they go to college? What do they like about their job and what do they hate? Do you know your employees' children? Their children's names? What activities they are involved in? What do their spouses or partners do for a living? What do they like to do on weekends? Are their parents alive? You need to know these things because these are the factors that motivate your workers to work. And these things impact their ability to perform at work.

Showing you care is harder for a boss to handle than anything else. Our concern for privacy has made us reluctant to get to know people. Big mistake. Although organizations do not forbid supervisors from getting to know their people, companies often broadcast the subliminal message that doing so somehow crosses some invisible line. The best managers ignore this subliminal message and get to know their people – not in a prying and intrusive way but in a way that enables them to understand what's important to their people. The things that are important to your people are the very things that motivate them to come into work day in and day out and get the job done for you.

People like to talk about what goes on in their lives, what frustrates them, what excites them and all kinds of other things. Listen to them. The insight they will provide into who they are will prove invaluable as you work with them in the future. That insight can be applied when deciding who to assign which projects or why productivity might be slipping in the last month. Most important of all, it makes your workers feel good that you listen, because your listening conveys that you care enough about them to take the time.

> Make it a point to learn one new thing every day about your people. In a year, imagine the insight you will have gathered, all of which will make you a better manager or supervisor.

Protect Your People

A willingness to protect your people needs to be at the heart of caring. Repeatedly, I refer to employees as "your people." They are yours to protect. They are the corporate equivalent of your flock and you are the shepherd. Your job is to keep them safe from the corporate wolves while at the same time making sure they do what they are expected to do.

Your people will come under attack from other managers or, often, from your own boss. Your job is to make sure they don't get "thrown under the bus." When something goes wrong, organizations look for someone to blame. People will make mistakes. Would a shepherd leave one of his sheep behind if it fell behind when a wolf was on the prowl? If you didn't answer with a resounding "no," then you need to take a good hard look at yourself as a leader. As a professional recruiter, I begin to salivate when I call people to try to recruit them just minutes or hours after their boss has thrown them to the wolves in a meeting. Their boss has just demonstrated how little they matter. The organizations and managers for whom I recruit don't do that, and I will tell prospective candidates just that. That is a huge selling point for most candidates. Why? Because too many bosses throw their people to the wolves.

Remember, ultimately, you are responsible for your people and what they do. You can't delegate responsibility for events that occur in your department. People know that and watch to see how you react to problems. Don't immediately look to someone else to assume the blame so you don't look bad. Accept responsibility and take the heat.

Your people will respect that. That respect will pay off big time when extra effort is required on a project or you are in need of that special touch only they bring to customer issues.

Never forget: When people are asked to rate the worst thing about their job, 75 percent say: their boss. If you are a lousy shepherd, you are in that 75 percent and your people will leave for greener pastures. If you become one of the unique group, one of the other 25 percent, imagine the competitive advantage you will have when you are trying to retain people!

- ▶ Caring is at the heart of being a *great* supervisor.

- ▶ People often quit because of the boss…not the company.

- ▶ If you know about your people's lives you will know what motivates them.

- ▶ Protect your people.

5

You Hire 'Em All... The Spouse, the Ex, the Kids and the Dog

LIKE IT OR not, we hire the husband, the kids, the dog and even the ex when we hire someone. And what affects each one of them also affects how your people perform on the job. Ask anyone who has a kid who's in trouble!

Remember, fully 20 percent of employees are experiencing some sort of issue in their life at any one time. Those issues have a real impact on the state of mind of your people when they are writing that software program... or not writing it because they are thinking about their daughter who is talking about moving in with that loser boyfriend of hers. The swiftness with which your organization can connect your people with the resources they need to get through various "bumps in the road" is critical in keeping your people fully engaged and productive. Helping people to do so also sends a very positive message: you truly do care. People never forget the supervisor or manager who is there for them, even if they might never admit it. When you help people through tough times, you become "human" in their eyes. It's much harder to walk out on a PERSON than it is to walk out on a nebulous entity like a "corporation."

I am also emphatic about the need for an Employee Assistance Program (EAP) that works. It needs to be more than some 800 number that people can call and get passed on to some unknown provider. The EAP needs to be sending people to resources that the EAP KNOWS will get the job done for your people. An organization's EAP should be performance-oriented. After getting someone's name, rank and serial number, one of the first questions should be is, "How is this affecting your work?" Makes sense right? After all, that's why you have them there. Is your EAP on the right track? A quick checklist of factors to consider includes:

> **Are the number of people who are accessing EAP realistic considering the size of your organization? (Low numbers mean your workforce has fewer issues**

than other organizations, right? NOT! If they are low, find out why!)

▶ Does EAP understand your environment and the problems your people face at work?

▶ Have the people answering the phone visited your workplace?

▶ Have they been briefed about your organization, its culture, and so on?

▶ Does your EAP provide people with mechanisms to cope *at work*? (People are going to have issues... but... they still have to function at work.)

Again, a positive EAP for your people sends the message that you care about them *as people*, at a time when the workplace is only becoming more depersonalized and most organizations view their people as a cog in the wheel. If you have an 800-number, strict quality assurance measures need to be in place to ensure it provides top-quality care. Initial contact can make or break an employee receiving prompt help and the right help for them to get back on track. When your people are focused and productive, it's good for business. And it's GREAT for your retention. Always remember one of my key rules of retention: PEOPLE TALK! You want them to be talking about how you helped them, their kids, their spouse, hey... maybe even their dog!

no nonsense notes

▶ If you don't care about people... get out of management!

▶ Protect your people in the same way a shepherd protects her flock.

▶ When you hire a person... you hire all of their baggage as well.

▶ Use an exceptional Employee Assistance Program. It's worth its weight in gold.

▶ People talk... Ensure they will be saying good things about you!

6

Accessibility and Approachability

GETTING OUT AND strolling around is the best way to make yourself accessible and you are far easier to approach when you pass right by someone. This habit makes it easy for people to stop you and ask you questions—questions they might never ask if they had to get up, walk into your office and disturb you. That's why the stroll is the best way to create accessibility... but it is not the only way.

You can also make yourself accessible when in your office. I am old school, from back in the day when people talked about having an "open-door policy" and literally meant they had an open door. If you had your door closed, you could expect the general manager to ask you why, and the answer better be a good one! Keeping your door open sends a powerful message; it tells your people that you are accessible. If they walk by and see your door open, they will be more likely to stop in and talk to you about something that is going on.

In addition to having an open door, NEVER situate your desk so that your back is to the door. It's as good as posting a sign that says, "Don't bother me." In one organization where I worked, the general manager sat with her back to the door, working on her computer all the time. She was the object of jokes because of it. And no one ever stopped in to talk to her. No one! She had no credibility and no one trusted her. It also set a tone for the rest of the organization and broadcast to other managers that it was perfectly okay to make yourself inaccessible.

Keep your door open at least 80 percent of the time. The only exception might be when you are engaged in a confidential meeting or call.

Part of making yourself accessible also includes not sending mixed messages about your accessibility. If your door is open, for example, but you are often on the phone or engaged in some activity, when employees stop by they may feel you are "busy." Don't let them leave. Signal to them that you would like them to wait. Motion them inside and invite them to sit down while they wait.

When employees stopped by and I was in the middle

of a call, I used to signal that I would quickly conclude the call by holding up one or two fingers. Then, if at all possible, I would conclude the call ASAP. These are *your people* we are talking about and they drive your success. They wouldn't be coming by unless they valued your opinion, needed you, or needed something. The message you send is powerful. They are more important than some person on the phone. If you make them wait, tell them who it was on the phone. Why? It's important to let them know why you kept them waiting. You wouldn't keep your boss waiting. Frankly, your people may be more important than your boss. There were times when I would tell my boss I would call her back because an employee was waiting to see me. THAT IS POWERFUL. You have just sent the message that your employee is more important than the boss. It makes the employee feel good about you and themselves. Your people drive your success and the success or your department, plant, office, etc. Success keeps the boss happy. Get it?

When you make employees wait or tell them to come by later, guess what happens? They stop coming by your office. It's like being rejected for a date; it's not long before people stop asking. More important, people rarely stop by just to chat. They need guidance, want your thoughts or need something in order to get their job done. Your lack of availability for employees has probably harmed individual productivity and created frustration among your people.

Being available for your people is like being available for your kids. When your kids need you, they need or want you AT THAT MOMENT, not 15 minutes from now. They are ready to talk. Talk to them, because if you don't, chances are when (or if) you do get back to them 15, 20 or maybe 45 minutes later, they have figured it out or don't want to talk anymore. The response you will get is something like this, "No big deal. It wasn't anything important." Do you *really* believe that? If you do, you're kidding yourself. It *was* important and you blew an opportunity to communicate because you weren't available. I hear people talk about quality time with their kids. That's a feel-good phrase to cover for the lack of time we spend with our kids overall. When my kids were young, I heard it said that *any time with your kids is quality time.* Your people are no different.

During my presentations, participants bring up the issue of having multiple locations all the time and ask how they handle that. The answer... visit those locations on a regular schedule. Once people get to know you, they will pick up the phone and call when they are faced with issues. Then, get back to them promptly. That's accessibility! You can use video conferencing and email to communicate, but there is no substitute for visiting your remote locations.

no nonsense notes

- ▶ Maintain a true open-door policy.

- ▶ Any time with your people is quality time.

- ▶ NEVER sit with your back to the door. It sends the message you are not accessible.

- ▶ Make time for your people. Avoid telling people to "come back later" when they come to your office.

- ▶ Your door should be open 80 percent of the time. Send the message that you are available and accessible to your people.

- ▶ Visit your remote locations regularly.

R✱E✱S✱P✱E✱C✱T
and Appreciation

RESPECT AND APPRECIATION are areas
that any leader has total control over. Your boss may
be a jerk and the organization may not value people to
the degree it should, but that doesn't mean that you
have to behave the same way. It certainly makes it
tougher if the organization is not in sync with you, but
it's not an obstacle that can't be dealt with.

Respect is about how you treat a person. Appreciation is about how you demonstrate to a person that you value what they do. The two can go hand-in-hand and merge, or they can be mutually exclusive. You can respect someone but take them for granted and fail to demonstrate your appreciation for their contributions to the organization or to you as a leader. We often know people respect us, even though we feel unappreciated. At a minimum, we owe people respect, but if you want to truly drive retention, *show* people you appreciate *and* respect them.

Respect. It's so basic to any human relationship that I shouldn't even have to write a section on the topic. Unfortunately, respect in the workplace has changed significantly in the past 30 years. Ironically, we talk about it more but show it less. Basic respect is about extending the simplest everyday courtesies. Respect is about character and class. Look at the people whom you respect. Ninety-nine percent of the time, the people you respect are people whom you feel possess character and class. You may not like them, but you do—sometimes, grudgingly—respect them.

And who do you guess most often tops the list of worst offenders when it comes to respect? In my opinion? The VPs, the presidents, the general managers and the owners. Yep. I hate to say it, but it's as if power and authority causes people to feel as if they have the right to behave in whatever manner they please. Maybe that's why so many people in these positions are viewed as arbitrary jerks. (I am being kind... if you are a senior-level executive or owner, your people use less kind terms to describe you in the hallway.)

Here is a simple test to determine whether or not your people respect you: Do you think that the first thing they talk about when they get home at night is *you*? If you are pretty sure that's the case, you have a problem! People who have a lousy boss need to vent immediately—to spouses, to significant others or to people who sit beside them at the bar. If they're talking about you first thing, you are probably not held in very high esteem!

One of your jobs as a leader is to set the tone within your "sphere of influence"... *And this is the area where you should start first.* The simplest way to set the tone and show respect is to say "hello" and say "good morning." Avoid sarcasm and barking out orders. And always make time for your people when they need to talk to you. Additional respectful behaviors are woven into every section of the book.

"Please" and "thank you." Using these words should be a very easy starting point. Use the words. Use them a lot. They go a long way in taking the edge off the requests we make of our people. People know you want or need something done yet we often act as if by using the words "please" and "thank you," we are somehow not communicating the urgency of the request. Much of it has to do with the fact that the pace of work has increased. We are more uptight and have simply become rude because of it. If you build a department or organization where you regularly use "please" and "thank you," you lay the foundation necessary to take respect to the next level.

In his book *The Fred Factor*, Mark Sanborn provides some of the best examples of the behavior that arises from a culture where "please" and "thank you" are evident. If you are a supervisor, applying the principles of *The Fred Factor* sends the positive message that you respect people. The best thing about it is... it feels good! Once it starts, people will pick up on it and you are on your way to building a positive feeling in your area of influence. I don't know about you, but I like to feel good... so why not try it...today. After reading this section commit

Start consciously saying "please" and "thank you" to-morrow... and keep tally to see how many times you do... this can become habit-forming!

to saying "please" and "thank you" and begin immediately... "please."

Also crucial to demonstrating your respect for people is avoiding jumping to conclusions. If an issue comes up, it is essential that you ask questions, listen to all sides of the story and *investigate.* Failing to do so sends everyone in your organization several negative messages:

- ▶ Their side of the story doesn't count.
- ▶ You already know the answer.
- ▶ You know more than they do.
- ▶ And, finally, you can't show the courtesy of getting their side of the story because you are the boss.

Result: You have just made huge strides in setting a tone of disrespect. That's in addition to risking a lawsuit or being hauled in front of the Equal Employment Opportunity Commission (EEOC) for a discrimination complaint because you didn't investigate before you acted... and reached the wrong conclusion!

Don't get me wrong—I am not saying don't discipline or fire people if they deserve it. Just make sure they deserve to be fired first. There have been countless times in my career in Human Resources that I have fired people and they have admitted they deserved it. They didn't like it but, regardless, I treated them with respect and the firing was far more positive. And guess what? Other people in the organization respected me because of the way I handled it. I always treat people with dignity and respect.

Ask yourself this question: How does your organization treat people when they resign to take another job? This also sends a powerful message to everyone else in the organization about whether or not you respect people. I often hear from candidates that they become lepers upon resigning, or, worse yet, are treated horribly. Your people are watching your every move and absorbing how you treat the people who are departing. Treating those who are departing shabbily is often the deciding factor for *other* people who are weighing whether or not they want to continue to work in your organization. As a recruiter, I get very nervous when companies treat people really well during their notice period. Why? Because people often start to feel sad about leaving those colleagues with whom they have good relationships. And that makes them vulnerable to a counter offer... or... more easily enticed back to that company at some point in the future if the new organization does not live up to their expectations. People are frequently counseled to avoid "burning your bridges" when leaving an organization. Likewise, organizations should never burn their bridges by treating a departing person poorly. (*For more information, you might want to take a look at the 10 Positive Behaviors from Wigwam Mills that are mentioned in Chapter 11 on Fear.*)

Showing appreciation is another matter. Often we take people for granted. We think that people should "know" that we appreciate what they do. When you are trying to retain people... why would you leave that to chance? SHOW people you appreciate them! TELL them you appreciate them! This is BASIC motivational theory... yet we fail to take advantage of the opportunity to use a FREE retention tool. In days of tight budgets, you need to be doing anything free that you can do.

Offer praise for a job well done. This can include a number of different forms of appreciation, including: acknowledging that you know someone stayed late to finish a project or letting people go home early on Friday because they have already put in 50 hours this week. Simple *gestures* such as showing your people that you value what they do for you. Notice I say "for you." Forget about the organization. Most people do things for you... not necessarily the organization but for you. You are the one who should show them appreciation. It is totally within your "sphere of influence."

There are hundreds of *gestures* that can demonstrate your appreciation to people. Google it on the internet and you will generate as many as you could possibly use. Pick ones that fit your style and incorporate them into your retention arsenal.

Before I leave the issue of showing appreciation, I want to touch on the most important way to show appreciation after the use of praise: Food! Personally, I am a big believer in food! Food seems to be the one thing everyone appreciates. It gets people mingling and breaks down barriers. "Breaking bread" together is a great way to show appreciation and create some camaraderie in your department, plant or company. Coming from Wisconsin I have found that bratwurst transcends all levels. In the southern U.S., it's barbecue. Hey... when in Rome do as the Romans do! Whatever you serve, food is one of the best ways to show your appreciation to your people for their accomplishments, for a job well done or for simply being a part of your team. Eating breaks down barriers and people begin to talk to one another as they would at home at the dinner table. When they talk... you listen... get to know them and build some trust. And remember, trust drives retention!

no nonsense notes

▶ Treat everyone with respect... always!

▶ Set a tone of respect within your "sphere of influence."

▶ Exercise common courtesy... Start by saying "please" and "thank you."

▶ Investigate prior to taking disciplinary action.

▶ Treat those who are leaving with respect.

▶ Praise is free. Use it to show your appreciation and to motivate.

▶ "Breaking bread" with your people transcends all levels in the organization... and it's better than eating a bologna sandwich for lunch!

8

It's Not About the Money... Not Totally

MONEY IS AN excuse. Managers and companies like to use it as an excuse when they are losing good people. It's a way to rationalize away all the things that they should be doing to retain people but are too inflexible or lacking in creativity or do not care about their people. This is reinforced by employees who, when they resign, will rarely tell the company the truth because they don't want to burn bridges. The line you always hear is: "I got a better opportunity for more money." When questioned they are evasive about their reasons or you receive a "vanilla" exit interview form.

Realistically, how many people are going to take a job for less money? Not too many people I know. If they do it's because you don't offer something in your environment. People leave for some other reason and get more money in the process. As a professional recruiter, it is very difficult for me to entice an employee away from their current job just because they are underpaid. If it's all about the money, people would accept a counter offer of more money from their current company every time. In my experience it only happens in about 5 percent of the time.

Pay

Don't get me wrong. Pay is important. Most of us are not independently wealthy and we don't work out of altruism. As you might have noticed, this book was not free! Studies that have been conducted since the beginning of time all bear this out. In most cases, money falls anywhere from third place to sixth place among reasons people leave their jobs. That being said, money is important. People work to pay the rent, cover the car payment, send the kids to college and allow them to do other things that add to their quality of life.

This is especially true with the millennium generation. They have been raised at a standard of living that is unprecedented in any workforce. Money is something they are used to having and, as a consequence, they are more driven by it than most generations. They like their toys, technology and their daily $5 mocha grande espresso lattes. They are also *more* driven by other factors *you* can control.

Another group to whom pay is more important includes those who earn less than $42,000 per year. People who fall in that bracket tend to be twice as likely to leave for money than those who earn more that $42,000 per year. Makes sense to me. Most people are trying to attain a standard of living that provides a reasonable level of comfort and pays for the things most of us want in life.

As much as it is possible, your goal is to reduce the importance of pay in the retention equation. Studies have shown that compensating people near what is average for their occupation or *slightly* above the average is ideal. If you aren't paying competitively, you better be doing everything else right. If you are paying competitively... you have just taken a major step to minimize the impact of compensation in the retention equation. When I used to propose this strategy, I used to immediately hear that it is a competitive market and that we have to watch costs closely. The key is to know what the market is paying for certain skills... then pay at the appropriate level *so you aren't underpaying* or *overpaying* by too much. Then communicate that to your people. This is particularly important today because people will go on the internet and pull up statistics of their own from places like salary.com, which I have found overstate what people are making. Beat them to the punch and have *accurate* statistics available. Show them the information and discuss it. That will help you to refute *their informal study*.

I especially want to point out one thing. Notice that I call it compensation, money or pay. That's how most people view it. My experience with employees is that if you want to irritate them... call it rewards! If you use the term, change it. People don't come to work to be rewarded, they come to get paid. I point this out because it speaks to how we communicate with employees. Most people hate buzz words and see them as ploys to distract them from the real issue as far as they are concerned, in this case, their pay!

Compensation, money or pay, whatever you want to call it, how you divide the compensation pie within the organization is crucial. This is as important as how much you pay. Nothing will drive an employee out of the organization faster than paying some slug the same (or close to the same) as a solid or great performer. Don't kid yourself. People have a pretty good idea what the person in the next cube is making and they compare their performance to that person's.

If you are a manager, *how you divide* the compensation pie is the one area that you most likely have a measure of control over. In most cases, you have a say in how you divide the pay pie at the end of the year... at least within certain parameters. Bottom line: Take the money from the lousy performers and give it to your solid and great performers. Unfortunately, most managers split the pie "equally" or pretty close to equally, thinking this will keep everyone happy. Sadly, according to a study done by the website World at Work (December, 2001), at most companies there's only about a 10 percent difference in what we pay our best performers and what we pay our average performers. Those top performers tend to outperform the average performers by 50 percent.

If you have great employees, you need to go to bat for them. Ask for more for them and be ready with a sound rationale *why it's good for business and the potential impact to the business if they leave.* The most that you can be told is "no." Then you know you have to use other tools to help retain that solid performer.

You shouldn't care if your slugs are happy or not. If they don't like it, let them leave... you will be better off. Your best people can always find another job. They're good and other companies recognize it. As an HR director, I rarely had a manager come in and say they wanted to take from the poor performers and give it to the good people. If they did, they never got an argument from me.

You should not be looking for equality... You should be looking for fairness. It IS fair to pay the solid performers more than lousy performers. After all, they are worth more to the organization. When that slug complains, take advantage of the opportunity to start a constructive dialogue about their performance. Tell them they got what they got because of their lousy performance, then tell them what needs to change if they want to see more money in the future. Discussions with lousy performers are not fun. Welcome to management. Don't weenie out! I would rather have that discussion than have to scramble to replace a top performer. THAT is not fun.

I also advocate overpaying people the business can't afford to lose. Yes... overpay. It comes down to a simple cost-benefit analysis. Risk vs. reward. Is it easy to swallow at times? No. Is it good business? Yes. I have seen more companies lose their top sales person because they refused to do this. This is the sales person who usually brings in 50 percent of the company's total sales. Then, the president or owner flips when they see the sales person's W-2 and realizes that they make more than the president himself. So they change the compensation plan to satisfy their ego and lose their best sales person to a competitor who WILL pay that sales person what they are worth. In the end, this costs the organization far more in lost sales and profits. Certain people you can't afford to lose... overpay those people.

If you want to develop a high performance organization and retain people in the process, your compensation plan needs to support attracting and retaining the BEST people. The best pay model for your business is one that Jim Collins points out in the book *Good to Great,* and one that Worthington Steel uses: Hire five people, work them like ten and pay them like eight. Take a guess what type of people you attract? People who want to BUST THEIR BUTTS! You get TOP performers because they can make more with your company than at other places and are willing to put out to get it. It's not what you pay them... it's what you get for what you pay them. This model is a magnet for high performers. You will also see that poor performers will be driven out of an organization like this by their co-workers or they will self-select out because they don't want to work that hard. Either way, you win as an organization. This is *the* best way to handle compensation from a retention and performance perspective. It is a great way to eliminate the money factor from the retention equation. It is also at the heart of building a high performing organization. More importantly, you have just put money on your bottom line if you are a CEO, GM or an owner. High performers pay for themselves.

Benefits

Studies have also shown that employees who are satisfied with their benefits are far more likely to stay. No surprise there... most people do realize the value of their benefits and mentally factor it in as a portion of the compensation they receive for the work they do. However, most people do not realize how big that portion is and that needs to be communicated to them. They also need to realize the impact on the bottom line to the organization. In many cases, they don't care. But most people, even the most stubborn ones, will grudgingly admit that a company has to make a profit so they can have a job.

When I worked in human resources, I always told employees to talk to their neighbors about what they're receiving by way of benefits and to come back in and tell me because I was curious to know what other companies were doing. Why would I encourage this? Because in the vast majority of cases, I was pretty sure that our benefits were better. Hey, I'd already researched the surveys and KNEW where we stood in the marketplace. I just forced the employees to do their own "market survey."

Picking the right benefits is imperative so you are not spending your money in the wrong places. First, analyze your workforce and find out what they value. Listen to what they are saying. People will talk. When they do, ask probing questions to understand what is important to them. Then, design your benefits structure around those needs so you are not wasting money to begin with. Each workforce is different. You need to be flexible and creative. Don't use a one-size-fits-all approach. I tell people that not everyone likes the same TV dinner. Personally, I like the $1 Banquet Salisbury steak TV dinner, with corn and mashed potatoes. I am not a fan of the turkey meal with the turkey, mashed potatoes and peas. If served the turkey dinner I will only eat the turkey and the mashed potatoes and throw the rest away. Benefits are the same way. Offer options on the various benefits so people can pick what they like. If you are doing that, you have taken a step to eliminate the attraction of another company's benefit plan as a factor in whether or not to leave. Employees are far more savvy today and take benefits into serious consideration when they are looking at job opportunities. An organization can spend a bundle of money on a high-end benefit plan, some of which certain employees may not even value. If you offer them the flexibility to pick and choose, you can offer more than the average without breaking the bank because you are not wasting money on benefits that they don't care about. In fact, offering flexibility in benefits is generally less expensive than a one-size-fits all benefit plan (*The*

Business Journal, "Benefits should fit employees of all ages" November 2, 2007).

Almost as important as the benefits you offer is the ease of access to those benefits. Ease of access and hassle-free usage is key. I have seen organizations with incredibly generous plans that people hated because they were difficult to access or when problems arose, nobody was there to help them solve the problem. Don't confuse "self-service" benefits with excellent service. In most cases we have moved to self-service and it could more aptly be described as "no service." The result: Employees who are not happy with their benefit plan do not see it as valuable and it does not have a positive impact on retention. If that's the case, you have just spent a huge amount of money and have gotten no retention benefit from a major cost item.

The answer to the dilemma is a solid benefit plan that is easy for your people to access with *help available if employees have a problem using it*! It doesn't get any simpler than that!

TIP

To see how you compare, pull out your most recent pay and benefits survey and spot check what you are paying several of your solid people. If you sense some issues, trust your gut and look to see if your pay and benefits are competitive... if not... take a look at the rest of your pay structure. (Note: If you don't have a pay and benefits survey... get one and start the process!)

One final note about pay and benefits or total compensation (not rewards!). Is your total compensation issue an easy one? Absolutely not. You need a carefully planned strategy that gives employees what they need. This will enable you to retain your best people and still

Check the differential in pay between your best performers and your average performers. Is it greater than 10
percent? If not, develop a plan to quickly to address it.

TIP

allow you to remain profitable. It is not as difficult as you
may believe and if done properly can effectively remove
"money" as a negative factor and, in many cases, give you
an advantage over your competition.

Flexibility

When deciding where to put this section I debated over
placing it after the "Benefits" section or after the "Caring"
section. That's because flexibility is a way of recognizing
that the lives of your people are hectic and that you as a
leader understand that. It also shows that by being flexible you care enough to work with your people to make
their lives easier. Most people view flexibility as a HUGE
BENEFIT! Your flexibility can be ad hoc or formal within the organization. According to a study conducted by
Hewitt Associates, 75 percent of the HR people see it as
a business tool that is in critical to retention, but only 46
percent of managers and 37 percent of executives do.

This topic recently came up in a round table of the
Talent Acquisition Committee in the Metro Milwaukee
SHRM chapter I attend. This group cited flexibility as the
chief driver in retention in an organization when faced
with limited or reduced budgets. It is also a perk that cuts
across generations, ethnicity and gender. In 25 years in
human resources, I have NEVER heard anyone complain
about having additional flexibility in their schedule.

The same Hewitt study mentioned above indicated that
managers tend to be the biggest determinant of whether
or not flexibility is allowed. Unfortunately, managers

tend to be paranoid about having to be equal or are worried about abuse so they avoid flexibility. Big mistake! In a time of limited budgets, flexibility has one huge advantage over other benefits... it's FREE. If you don't give it a try, how will you know if you are throwing out a no-cost retention tool? And, the reality is that most organizations do not put severe restrictions on a manager's ability to be flexible within your department. Why? What do most organizations care about? RESULTS. If you are getting the results senior management needs, they are not going to place severe restrictions on you. The question should be not whether or not you should allow flexibility but instead, "If I allow flexibility, will it enable me to get better results while helping me to retain my best people?" If you start to get better results, do you really think the president is going to pick up the phone and chew you out because you let someone leave early to go to the doctor?

If you are in human resources, you need to be pointing out that people see this as a major benefit and that RESULTS are what matter to senior management. As an HR person, you need to make sure you don't get paranoid and tie the hands of your department managers. Allow them to use this powerful tool! Monitor it to ensure abuse is not occurring... or better yet... help your managers find ways that will enable them to use the tool effectively.

Let's quickly address the issue of the complainer who says "You aren't being fair!" My question to the complainer is whether or not they are getting their job done. Chances are they aren't! If they aren't, that's probably one of the reasons you don't offer them the flexibility that you offer to the better performer. I used to handle this in a simple way when I was in HR. I would tell them the truth. They aren't getting the flexibility because they aren't getting the job done. This discussion may wake them up. By having the discussion you have also taken another major step in retention by starting to deal with their lousy performance. If they don't like it and quit... you now have an opportunity to hire someone who will perform up to expectations.

Flexibility can take many different forms, including allowing employees to:

▶ Leave early or come in late so they can deal with personal issues.
▶ Work different hours in summer.
▶ Work a compressed work week, such as four ten-hour days. (My experience is that once people go to this schedule you will have a war on your hands if you try to go back to the standard five eight-hour days.)
▶ Work from home all of the time or on certain days.
▶ Take their vacation time in increments smaller than half-days.

This is a short list... a very short list. *Flexibility is only limited by your imagination and your desire to try it!*

Sit down with one or two of your fellow managers and discuss areas where you are currently allowing your people flexibility and discuss new areas where you could allow additional flexibility. THEN... have each manager try a new one!

TIP

Goal Alignment and a Greater Good

Goal alignment is an intangible that many organizations neglect. If your employees' goals are in alignment with the company's goals, employees are far more likely to stay because if they leave, they are abandoning the *mission*. By doing so, they have made a conscious decision to abandon something which they have believed in for years. It's far less likely that they will abandon a "belief" than quit a *job*.

The best examples of goal alignment in organizational retention include the United States military and non-profit organizations. In both cases, people are not staying because of the money. They stay because they believe in the mission of the organization; they are working for something more than money. Their personal goals are intertwined with the mission of the organization. Clearly, no one in the military does it simply for the money.

Another great example of goal alignment and the greater good exists within the Toro Company. Retired CEO and president Ken Melrose recast the company as an "environmental" company. The people weren't just making lawn mowers, they were making products that were environmentally friendly. I knew the HR manager at their large lawn mower plant in Tomah, Wisconsin, and he would have done anything for the company. That attitude pervaded the workforce because they felt they were contributing to the "greater good" by making environmentally responsible products. As a result, turnover was minimal there even before "going green" was vogue.

Can every organization find a mission that people can latch onto that is for the greater good? I believe they can... at least to some extent. Get creative and ask yourself: What does your organization do that makes a difference? Me... I take pride in matching people with companies and making a difference in people's lives by propelling their careers forward, not just finding a "body" to fill an open job requisition for a client company. That goal alignment makes it a lot easier to get up in the morning and to work into the evenings interviewing potential candidates. It was one factor that kept me from bailing during the first three years of my business, when times were tight. People in larger organizations are no different.

Develop a list of ways that your organization makes a difference in people's lives or adds to the greater good. Then identify a strategy to convey this to your people. (Ideally, you will do this with several of your managers.)

no nonsense notes

▶ Money isn't the main reason they quit.

▶ Studies show that money is more important to people who earn less than $42,000 per year.

▶ Hire five people... work them like ten... pay them like eight... you will make money in the process.

▶ Pay your people fairly... that means top performers get paid more than average performers!

▶ One size *doesn't* fit all when it comes to benefits. Offer your people choices when at all possible.

▶ A flexible schedule is one of the most prized benefits you can offer your employees.

9

Help Them Grow...
and Flourish

WHEN I TEACH a class, I tell my students that people are like tomato plants. You should see the odd looks I get... at first. You can plant tomatoes in your garden and do nothing else except leave it up to Mother Nature. Sometimes the plants grow, if you are lucky enough to get rain and the weeds don't stunt the growth of the plants. But we all know there is a better way. Water the plants, weed the garden and perhaps even fertilize it. Then what do you get? A more prolific garden with better tomatoes! Well, PEOPLE ARE LIKE TOMATOES. If you give them some attention, they will grow... and thrive.

How many people out of a hundred really know what they want in their career? I dare say, not a whole lot! Encourage your people to think about their careers, especially your young people. Most young people coming out of school have no clue what they want to do in their careers. I know I really didn't even though I thought I did. In many cases, their parents don't know. If parents do know, it's unlikely their kids will listen to them? I have spoken with hundreds of people about their careers. I'm also the parent of two college kids. Do you think that my kids listen to Dad? (Maybe a little but not nearly as much as they should.) Your people are more likely to listen to YOU, as their boss, than anyone else because their paychecks are impacted by you.

Encourage people to think about their careers in the context of their lives. Until about six years ago, I never did. Then one day, simply by accident, I stumbled onto Jeffrey Gitomer's *Little Gold Book of YES! Attitude*. With it, I began a journey that has led me to books by authors Jim Rohn, Tony Robbins and dozens of others. Then I actually laid out a game plan. The game plan has led to planning and building for the future and I realized that I had wasted many years of my life for lack of a life plan... My career is only one piece of the plan. If you can get your people thinking about their careers in the context of their lives, they will develop a sense of purpose, be more driven, accomplish more and be far happier in their jobs. Who reaps the benefits? Certainly they do... but so do you! It enables you to help them perform better and prepare to take that next step in the organization. In my experience, young people often leave jobs too early because they do not feel as if they are growing or are going somewhere. They usually are...they just don't know it. It's your job as a manager to point that out to them OR, if they aren't going anywhere, point them in the right direction. I recently recruited an engineer with great potential who felt his company had no plans for him. Even though they had alluded to him that he would play a role in the future expansion of the consulting firm, they had never REALLY talked to him about their thoughts. After he gave his notice, they suddenly started to lay out all the specific ideas they had for him. Too late... his mind was made up and he is now a member of an organization that has instituted developmental plans for its people.

In many organizations, there is no room for promotion because they are too small or upward advancement is not available. But there is ALWAYS room for people to grow. By helping people continue to grow, you will retain people far longer than if you neglect them. In a study done by Sibson Consulting it was found that "work content is always the largest motivator of good performance and the most consistent driver of retention, regardless of age." Eventually the person who values "growth" may leave anyway, but... if they feel they are growing, they are far more likely to stick around a bit longer. Just because the organization does not have a formal plan to help people grow does not mean you as a department manager can't have growth plans for your people. Be the exception! When other department managers lose their sharpest talent every two years, you will keep yours for three or perhaps four years. You have just doubled the retention rate of everyone else.

Career development is not only for the young. As people progress in their careers, they still want to know where they are going. Even if they have no desire to be promoted, most people love to take on new challenges to avoid boredom. When boredom sets in, people get restless and begin to wonder if the grass isn't greener on the other side of the fence. Keeping these people in place and engaged is a way to strengthen your department and to avoid the instability created by turnover. The people who serve you longer can prove to be the people who will sustain you in difficult times.

The easiest way to get the ball rolling on developing your people is to ASK them what they want. Most times, they will not be able to tell you. If they do, that's great. Then you can work with them to make sure their expectations align with your department and company goals. By asking them, you have put the ball in their court and they will do most of the work. After all... it's their career. You just have to be there to provide support and assist them in *their* growth. Your job is not to take ownership of their plan. Your job is to get them thinking and planning. You can also monitor whether they are acting on their plan. *This does not have to be some big fancy process.* ASK them, discuss ideas, develop ways to help them get there and show them how they can put the plan into action. It's simple. I like it simple.

In his book *Leadership: Thinking, Being, Doing* (WME Books, 2007), Lee Thayer outlines a leader's obligation to prevent his people from defaulting on themselves. By asking questions and expecting your people to act on what they develop, you prevent them from defaulting on their career and in many cases their lives. By expecting them to perform, you help people to optimize their potential.

- ► ASK your people what they want.

- ► People are like tomatoes... they won't grow if they don't get nourishment.

- ► Growth can occur within your job or within the company.

- ► Top performers will not tolerate a lack of growth.

- ► Work content is a consistent driver of retention regardless of age.

no
nonsense
notes

Expect Performance: Fire Your "Slugs"

THIS AREA TOPS the list of those in which most managers and organizations tend to fail. They don't manage performance regularly or tell people what they expect from them. If they do tell them what they expect, they often fail to hold them accountable when they don't do what's expected. Instead, they wait and tolerate substandard performance until frustration hits the breaking point. Then they bring the offending employee into their office and fire them. THAT IS NOT THE WAY TO DO IT!

There is nothing that irritates employees more than having to carry non-performers. Want to take a huge step forward in retention? FIRE YOUR SLUGS. That's it. Real simple. The people who work with them will love you as a boss and...more importantly... respect you! Unfortunately, organizations have become paranoid about firing people. Don't get me wrong, when you fire someone it should be with good reason. The problem should be properly investigated, documented and, ultimately, the termination should be done with the utmost dignity and respect. Nonetheless... your slugs need to be fired, not only from a business perspective but also from a retention perspective.

You have an obligation to the organization and to your people to do it right. In many cases, managers allow people to default on themselves and let them get away with non-performance. Then one day they get fed up and fire them. That's not the way to do it. Not only do you look like an arbitrary jerk... you may very well get hauled into court in today's litigious society. The process is simple. Here it is.

- ▶ Tell your people what you expect from them.
- ▶ Give them the tools and support they need to get the job done.
- ▶ If they don't meet your expectations, bring them in and TALK TO THEM... Ask them questions and help them problem-solve to get back on track.
- ▶ If they don't solve the problem, terminate them... with dignity and respect!

Terminating someone is never easy. If it ever does become easy for you, it's time to get out of management because you have probably become callous and uncaring.

▶ Tell people what you expect from them and hold them accountable for their performance.

▶ Fire your slugs... Your good performers will love you!

▶ Terminations should be handled with dignity and respect... always!

no nonsense notes

Drive Negativity and Fear Out of Your Environment

NEGATIVITY AND FEAR are the two emotions most likely to suck the life out of your organization. It's one thing not to have fun at work. It's another to have negativity.

Negativity can be driven by such things as:

- ▶ Pessimistic leadership.
- ▶ Tolerance of negative behavior or—worse yet—rewards for it.
- ▶ Lack of appreciation.
- ▶ Lack of control over your job.
- ▶ Lack of challenge.
- ▶ No one listening to you.
- ▶ Slow, inaccurate or incomplete information.
- ▶ Excessive workload.

This list is from a presentation by Julie Kowalski called *Breaking Free of Workplace Negativity*, which she gave at a seminar I attended in 2010. The thing about this list that should jump out at you is that managers can impact every one of these items to some extent, excessive workload to a lesser extent, perhaps, than the others. But the rest of the list can be successfully influenced by any manager of an area. When I hear the managers' mantra: "I have no control over that," I want to scream. I used to hear those excuses all the time. Stop making excuses and start having an impact.

It starts with you as a manager. You set the tone for your "sphere of influence." If you complain and moan when a directive comes down from higher up in the organization, you need to stop doing so immediately. It is demoralizing to your people, even if they seem to agree with you. They know you shouldn't be doing it so it diminishes your stature as a leader in their eyes. Worse yet, it sends the message that negativity is acceptable.

When negativity becomes a part of a culture, it will be reflected in how people communicate to customers, the level of quality that is achieved and the atmosphere that prevails within the organization. When you tour a negative organization, you can smell the stench of decaying morale. You can feel it in the atmosphere. No one wants to come to work, much less take care of the customer.

If you have negative people in your organization, you need to deal with those people. Sit down with them and explain what type of behavior you expect and why. When you see them displaying negativity, you need to call them on it and tell them the positive behavior you expect. If you are in a leadership position and you see a more junior member of your management team engaged in negative behavior, address it IMMEDIATELY. If they do not change, get rid of them.

Negative people will also sour even the best new hire. It seems that the negative people have to find someone to associate with... probably because nobody else will associate with them. What do these negative people do when you hire a new person? They immediately attach themselves to the new hire and poison their thinking by telling them how evil the organization is, how lousy it is to work there, that the management team consists entirely of jerks and on and on and on. They indoctrinate new people with their own beliefs about how bad the place is. (To find out how to handle new hires correctly, see Chapter 13 on orientation and mentoring.)

Lead by example. *Don't add to negativity by ignoring this behavior or by engaging in it.* To do so is like seeing a wildfire and either letting it burn or throwing gas on it; both are clearly the wrong thing to do. Unconsciously,

Before you say anything negative about something, say two positive things about the situation first. This will immediately begin to shift your thought process... and ultimately your behavior... toward a more positive leadership approach.

TIP

you may find yourself agreeing with negativity or joining in. First and foremost, ensure that you never fall into that trap. You may not like having to do something, but you need to keep that to yourself. Bite your tongue. If you don't, you may undermine the entire leadership structure. Unfortunately, society keeps telling people that management is all screwed up and doesn't care. Your people are bombarded with movies like "Office Space," "The Devil Wears Prada," and comic strips like "Dilbert" which all depict management in a negative light. As a member of the management team, you have to counteract that because negativity makes your organization a less desirable place to work and negatively impacts your ability to retain people.

I have seen organizations successfully purge themselves of negative behavior. It wasn't easy, but in each case the company realized that it was necessary. In one case, in Sheboygan, Wisconsin, at Wigwam Mills (they make the best socks in the world, by the way), union and management tackled it together. They met and developed a list of ten positive behaviors that were expected of everyone, regardless of their position in the organization or their union status. It was stressed that this wasn't about union or management, it was about individual behavior. The development of this list sent a strong message to everyone that negative behavior was not acceptable. It worked.

People began to hold each other accountable for not adhering to the ten positive behaviors. Management was held to a higher standard. The president expected the management team to lead by example.

Check out this list on the facing page. There is nothing earth-shattering about it. They did it as a company. You can do it as the head of your department, team, facility or division. You can do it in your "sphere of influence."

10 Positive Behaviors

1   **Show respect** by being courteous and tactful toward others.

2   **Be responsible** by keeping your commitments and being on time.

3   **Enthusiastically cooperate** with others by following procedures, being willing to learn, knowing your job, being receptive and approachable, being open minded and becoming a team player.

4   **Communicate well** by using appropriate language, praising others and being a good listener.

5   Do your best to **be friendly** and exhibit a good sense of humor.

6   **Be supportive** of the successes of others and show concern and caring to your fellow employees.

7   **Use your time well**; be neat, clean and organized.

8   **Be honest and truthful** with yourself and others.

9   Work to your **greatest potential.**

10 **Be fair** in everything you do.

One final word on negativity. After you have stopped the cycle of negativity... and *you can stop the cycle...* you need to start rewarding the people who exhibit positive behavior. *When you do that... you will start the spiral moving upward instead of downward!*

Develop your own list of positive behaviors with your team, department or facility. Then, put them in writing and post them where they will be visible to everyone and start holding each other accountable to them. Positive behaviors snowball quickly! (Trust me... you will quickly change once your people start calling you on not following the behaviors. They expect you to lead by example.)

Fear

Fear arises primarily from three sources:

▶ Uncertainty about the organization's direction and the potential impact on a person's position.

▶ People being punished for taking initiative and making mistakes.

▶ A boss or other senior leadership person who uses fear as a tool to run their area of influence.

In all cases, the result tends to be the creation of an aversion to risk taking. Everyone is afraid to say or do whatever he or she requires in order to do the best job possible. They play it safe. Then one day, everyone wakes up, finds they can't keep good people or the business has fallen into mediocrity and it's in a death spiral.

Uncertainty about the organization's direction is the easiest to deal with. The answer? Communicate with your people. Now wasn't that easy? A well thought out communications strategy is THE best way to effectively drive communication. Don't do it in a haphazard way. Sit down, strategize and develop a well layered approach using *multiple types* of communication. By doing so, you ensure that everyone will hear the message multiple times and in different media. Use the following list and you will cover 95 percent of what needs to be covered without having some big fancy system that looks great but wastes time and probably doesn't get through to employees anyway.

- ▶ Managers and leaders at all levels need to get out into the cube factory or on the plant floor and start talking with people *daily*.
- ▶ Have an open door so people come in and ask questions.
- ▶ Hold departmental meetings that provide a consistent message, a forum for ideas and a place to bring up concerns about the functioning of the department.
- ▶ Hold company-wide, plant-wide or division-wide meetings that focus on what is going on in the business, plans for the future and how well the business is doing.
- ▶ Develop regular postings and updates using email, company intranet or written notices.

A quick note on meetings: Everyone thinks that when I mention meetings that I am talking about long drawn-out events. Only if you let them be long and drawn out! They can range from five minutes to an hour depending on what you want to accomplish. Frankly... 90 percent of the meetings that last an hour or more are just people rambling on, in my experience. Keep meetings short, sweet and to the point. The goal of every meeting should be *educating* people and *generating actions that drive results*! Information and education will eliminate fear... and drive understanding of what it takes for the business to succeed. Both of which reduce turnover and improve how the business operates as well. RETENTION DOES NOT EXIST IN A VACUUM... IT'S AIDED BY DRIVING ORGANIZATIONAL SUCCESS!

TIP

If you are not holding regular meetings that 1. educate and 2. generate results... start! Then... ask yourself at the end of each meeting if you have accomplished those two objectives.

This is the meat and potatoes. Anything beyond these two points is pure gravy. When you get information out and educate your people, you will virtually shut down any negative influence from the internal grapevine. By doing so, you eliminate speculation, uncertainty and self-serving communication. When you do that... you have just significantly reduced several major sources of FEAR. The beautiful thing about this approach... even if you are only a supervisor or manager... is that you can do most of these things within your "sphere of influence." So even if the organization chooses not to do some of these things, you can still have an impact!

In recent years, experts have begun using the term "bullying" to describe what I would call "fear." It is an abusive pattern of behavior that creates uncertainty and a nagging sense of fear in an employee's mind. Call it fear or bullying, the effect is the same. It kills optimal performance and drives turnover. It's that simple.

Fear is something that rarely pervades the entire organization. More often than not, it is found in pockets of the organization where a toxic boss has been allowed to act with impunity or is politically astute and hides his or her tactics of leading by fear. Unless the organization deals with this manager, the organization risks sending the damaging message to *all* employees that it is willing to condone inappropriate managerial behavior. The people in other departments will then wonder if the organization would also look the other way if this happened to them.

By not dealing with an abusive boss the organization looks clueless or... worse yet... seems to condone this behavior. This can prove to be a decision point for a person weighing whether or not to leave. It plants the seed in an employee's mind that the organization simply does not care about people in general. Mentally, a person will use this as a way to rationalize moving, even if they work for a good boss. It makes it easier to turn in that resignation when offered another job.

The unfortunate thing about fear is that it often originates with a key person in the organization, such as the head of a division, a plant manager or a vice president who is successful. These people hide behind mantras like: "I expect the best from my people and that's why they don't like me," or "They quit because they couldn't stand the pressure," or the best of all. "I provided them with a great training ground so now they are able to take that next step in their career." When people see a senior-level person getting away with ruling by fear, they will have an inherent distrust of the organization. They will not openly express their thoughts, but they will when talking with their co-workers, when out to lunch, or having a drink after work. There will be a very low buzz in the organization. If you are looking for open comments to verify high level fear before addressing a problematic senior-level person, you will never address the problem because people aren't dumb enough to commit political suicide openly.

How do you know you have a problem?

▶ **The best people who work under this person are leaving... They don't have to put up with this... and they won't!**

▶ **You get guarded or very carefully-worded responses**

to questions about what is going on in that division
or area.
- ▶ Again and again the buzz is that someone is a "jerk."
  (I am being kind because the words they will use are
  often sandwiched between a few expletives.)
- ▶ VERY slight innuendo is made when people talk
  about how that department is run.
- ▶ Employees request transfers to other areas of the
  organization.
- ▶ A good employee leaves and they will be "too busy"
  to fill out the exit interview form.

On a rare occasion, you may have a good employee
leave, transfer or outright quit without another job, and
they will walk into your office, unload on you and tell
you that they are telling you this with the understanding
that it is "off the record" and do not want it being shared
because they do not want to burn any bridges.

Ask yourself if any of the above situations have occurred
in your organization. If they have, start asking questions
about them because chances are, you have a problem.

In most cases, the only way you will know there is
a problem is that you will get bits and pieces of all of
the above. A great big jigsaw puzzle will begin to come
together. Slowly, you will see the picture, though there
always seems to be a few missing pieces. At that point,
you have a tough decision. (That's why they pay you the
big bucks!). Look the other way or take some action to
address the issue decisively.

If you are in tune with your people, you will see the
signs all along, so the puzzle will take shape over time.

Ideally, you will bring issues forward to the people who need to know about them. Hopefully, they will step in, communicate decisively with the problematic manager and the manager will change his or her behavior. If they are unwilling or unable to do so, I suggest you start questioning whether or not it is the type of organization YOU want to work in!

As a department manager, you may have to deal with a boss who uses bullying or fear as a way to manage. Your job, whether you like it or not, is to insulate your people from your boss. If you don't, you will bear the brunt of dealing with the aftermath of the turnover your boss generates.

no nonsense notes

▶ You set the tone in your "sphere of influence."

▶ Deal with your negative people... Change them or remove them!

▶ Tell your people the behaviors you expect from *every one of them*.

▶ Communicate in multiple ways and at multiple levels to optimize communication.

▶ Keep your meetings short!

▶ Meetings are designed to educate and to drive results.

▶ Deal with toxic managers... Where there is smoke, there is usually fire.

Hire the
Right People

FACE IT, HIRING is often done when someone quits and the organization is under the gun to replace a person quickly because organizations no longer carry excess people. With no fat to pick up the slack, managers rush to get a "body" to fill a hole. Managers do not evaluate the skills they truly need to fill the role and therefore do not capitalize on a golden opportunity to pick the best candidate.

Would you buy a piece of equipment that cost $180,000 without thoroughly going over specifications and what you needed that piece of equipment to do? No way! I remember arguing for hours in a staff meeting about the features we wanted on a new coffee maker! If you hire someone and pay him $30,000 per year and expect him to stay with the organization even for only three years, you have just decided to invest $180,000 in a human asset. I don't know about you... but when I purchase something for $180,000, I do my homework. I know what I need and the means with which I will evaluate if it is the right piece of equipment. Hiring people should be no different!

There is a simple way to make sure you get the right people... Use a systematic approach that employs the following elements.

- ▶ Know what you need.
- ▶ Train the people who are involved in the selection process.
- ▶ Assess candidates for fit... not just for skills.
- ▶ Don't over-hire.

Know What You Need

If you determine the skills you "must have" and the skills you "want to have," you will know it when you see it. The belief that you have to interview some predetermined number of people is ludicrous. This isn't a shopping trip to the mall where you are looking for a pair of pants and have only a slight idea of what you want. You should KNOW before you start that you want gray pants of a certain waist size, length, fabric and so on. This is crucial to you recognizing the right candidate when they walk in the door. If the right candidate comes in... and you decide to look at three more because this is the first one... chances are that person will be gone by the time you get done finding, scheduling and interviewing the other three people. Happens all the time. Why? Good people will be snatched up by companies that are decisive and know a great candidate when they see one. As important as the retention component is, also remember that while your job sits vacant... things are not getting done that are costing you money!

Train the People Involved in the Selection Process

Sadly... most interviewees are better prepared and more knowledgeable than the people conducting the interview. Answer this question honestly: Have you ever gone through any formal interview training? Has anyone taught you how to prepare for an interview? How to listen to the responses of candidates? I ask these questions all the time when I conduct my "No Nonsense Retention" presentation. Generally, only 20 percent of the people answer that they have received formal interview training. Yet every candidate in the world is reading articles on job boards, and practicing and learning how to respond appropriately to questions. Practice does make perfect and most candidates are pretty good.

Although people can learn to interview by learning on the job... it certainly isn't optimal. Everyone requires at least some *baseline* training to get on the right path. Once that has been accomplished, start to monitor your newly trained interviewers. Observe and correct their performance. Once they feel comfortable you will see the difference in how they conduct an interview. For that matter... if you are in HR... get out of there and get some formal training yourself!

Don't Over-Hire

You are not looking for God in a three-piece suit! It's great to get a candidate who has everything you "want"...and then some. The problem is... why would this person want your job? And... if they do take the job, how long would they stay? Often we see a great candidate who brings more to the table than we actually need. As mom used to say, "If it's too good to be true... it probably is." Occasionally that magnificent candidate will come along and it works out well... but not usually.

Over-hiring leads to many of the retention issues we have talked about: unrealistic desire to grow, fairness, pay, and so on. When these issues are all mixed together, you are faced with a no-win retention issue. You will expend extensive time and energy dealing with an issue you could have avoided by hiring a person who meets the needs that you have. If it seems too good to be true... it probably is!

Hire for "Fit"... Not Just for Skills

Last, and most importantly, you need to be looking for "fit." Studies show that fit is the most important determiner of success on the job... not whether or not they are familiar with Excel, SAP or have a masters degree. "Fit"... or chemistry... is what you are after. Chemistry is not if they know Excel or SAP. Fit is about those *traits* that are crucial to a person's ability to mesh with their boss, co-workers and the culture of the organization. Unfortunately, interviewing is one of the least reliable ways to determine fit... even if your interviewers are trained and conduct proper interviews.

I encourage all of my clients to use some form of psychometric testing instrument to help determine fit... whether it is for various traits of personality, ability to learn or mental horsepower. The instruments have become incredibly accurate as they have evolved through the years. They "strip away the veneer" so that an organization gets a look at the real person and... combined with solid interviewing, can enhance your ability to determine fit. By using an instrument, you have just eliminated one more uncertainty that can lead to a poor hire... and... ultimately, turnover.

A good friend of mine who specializes in providing these instruments to organizations, uses a Brannock Device (that's the thing you put your foot in at the shoe store to measure your foot size) to illustrate how important fit is to the success of a new hire. You can get a size 8 foot in a size 7 shoe for a period of time, but after a while your feet start to hurt because they do not fit! Just like a person. Most candidates, like politicians, put their best foot forward to get the job... then... after about six to nine months they can no longer be someone they aren't and their real personality comes out. His point: If you are lucky, your organization is a size 7 and so is the candidate. If not, you and the new hire may rub each other the wrong way. Sometimes the fit is close and all is well... if not, you have just built turnover into your hiring process.

Another advantage of using a psychometric testing instrument is that it gives you incredible insight into how the new person "ticks." The result: you have now reduced the time it takes for the boss and the new person to get to know each other and have also eliminated one element that can slow the ramp-up time to productivity. If you are REALLY intent on ensuring the right fit... have the boss take the instrument as well and let the boss and new person share their results with each other. Do it during the hiring process! What this does is help each party to understand why they act the way they do. It also helps the boss best manage the new person. The psychometric testing instrument is your "owner's manual." Would you buy a $180,000 piece of equipment and let the equipment supplier drop it off without an owner's manual? No way!

There is another huge benefit to both parties knowing what makes each other "tick." Remember... 75 percent of the people in this country say the worst thing about their job is their boss, right? If the candidate knows what they are getting going into the relationship... they may see they are a bad "fit" and not take the job either. Again... unnecessary turnover is reduced. If you think I am nuts... ask yourself how the guy who runs eHarmony has made MILLIONS of dollars. He uses psychometric testing instruments to measure compatibility (i.e., "fit") to make good matches. When I realized that was no different than looking for the right fit in a new hire, I started using these instruments as an HR guy... and I now advocate them to the clients for whom I conduct professional search assignments. Why? THEY WORK!

The formula for reducing your turnover on the front end is increased by:

▶ Knowing the type of person you want in the job.
▶ Training the people who are interviewing.
▶ Avoiding over-hiring.
▶ Using psychometric testing instruments to assess for fit.

Schedule some interviewer training in the next two months. Get someone who knows how to interview to conduct the training if you are not that person. Result: The people who have to conduct the interviews will be more confident and competent.

Go online and look at some of the psychometric testing instruments that are available and try some of the
demos to find one that is right for your organization.

TIP

Diversity of Thought

For years we have heard about how the generations
all have a different thought process on how they view
work... and life for that matter. People lament that the
new generation does not want to work as hard but instead
works to live and not lives to work. I actually started to
write a section on the generations and was convinced by
my wife and youngest son not to. Why? Because it is our
experiences that impact us... not our generation. For example... the myth that "old people" (like me) are not technologically savvy is ridiculous. I have seen people my
age who are better technologically than people in their
twenties. It's also a myth that people in their fifties want
to coast to retirement. I hear that a lot when companies
say they want someone who will be with them longer so
they don't want someone over fifty. Pleeeeaaaasssse! It's
not the age... it's the fire in the belly. I work harder than
90 percent of the population because I have that fire even
though I am in that over-fifty crowd.

Forget about age/generation, race, sex, accent, sexual
orientation and so on. What people think is the key.
I don't know about you, but the last time I checked I
couldn't read minds and don't know anyone that can.
So... ask your people what they think, what they value,
how important work-life balance is to them and where
they see their career going. Assumptions based on some
trait are what get us in trouble when building our retention tower. Flexibility in your approach is what is needed

because the one thing that is true in today's workforce is that we are more diverse. Our different thoughts about work and so on are what drives whether or not we stay with an organization, how many hours we want to work in a week, if we value certain benefits, and more. Your understanding of those thoughts is the starting point in building your retention tower.

Listen to your people and be flexible... That's how you will be able to effectively deal with a diverse workforce. Is it EASY? No. However, it's easier than you think if you talk to your people, listen to them and act based on the information you hear from them.

no nonsense notes

- ▶ Know what you "must" have and what you "want" to have in a candidate... and be realistic.

- ▶ Fit is THE most important determiner of success on the job... Hire for fit not just for skills.

- ▶ Train anyone that participates in the interview process on how to conduct an appropriate interview.

- ▶ Use psychometric testing instruments to improve your ability to find someone with the proper fit.

- ▶ Ask your people what's important to them... You can't read minds!

- ▶ Flexibility is a must when determining which retention tools are important to a diverse workforce.

Orientation: Winning Their Hearts and Minds

THE GOALS OF an orientation are simple... *Real Simple!*

- ▶ Assimilate the person into the organization.
- ▶ Make them productive as quickly as possible.
- ▶ Educate them about the organizational culture and values.
- ▶ Complete the necessary paperwork to comply with the law, get people paid and enroll them in benefits programs.

When it comes to retention, the first three are *the* most important. Unfortunately, most organizations have orientations that appear to be targeted to completing the last item. ORIENTATION IS NOT ALL ABOUT COMPLETING THE PAPERWORK!

A major reason for having a systematic, gradual and well-thought-out orientation is to assimilate the person into the organization. Your goal is to assimilate the new employee into the culture, to familiarize them with the values and goals of the organization and to establish expectations. This is the time that the organization truly has the employee's ear... they are listening and want to hear what the organization is all about. If you don't fill that void... who will? Answer: The worst employee in the place, the one who complains and moans about everything. They attach themselves to new employees like leeches in a swamp and begin sucking the life out of them. If you don't fill the communication void... someone will (and it's usually some loser!)

Here is the typical first day in most places. Several hours with the HR administrator filling out paperwork and being given the handbook to sign. Forget about reading the thing, much less understanding the key points... just sign it so we have something for the file! If the newbie is lucky, she will have an office ready and be set up with a computer, email account, phone system and at least a stapler and some office supplies. In an age of high-tech software, digital systems and advanced manufacturing techniques, this is an absolute *must* to get new employees up to speed and allow them to become a productive member of the organization as soon as possible. It's difficult enough coming into a new organization where you don't know anyone much less not have the BASIC tools needed to get the job done.

The new employee shakes their head and wonders what type of organization they have joined when a lousy orientation takes place. You can hear this sucking sound as all the positive energy, excitement, and enthusiasm about the new job that existed prior to starting is drained from that employee. A lousy orientation is incredibly moronic from a productivity perspective but also from a retention standpoint.

You expend all of the time and effort to attract and land top talent but then just throw them in and let them learn as they go. There is no organized plan or there's one that, on its surface, appears organized but fails to take into account that a person can only absorb so much in one day. It is the classic example of putting 10 pounds of poop in a 5 pound bag! *People can't sit through 8 hours of orientation!*

People are nervous, scared and uncertain for the first few days on the job. Their anxiety level is at an all time high. They are extremely vulnerable to counter offers from their former employers. Face it... counter offers are a major problem when bringing a new employee on board. Often organizations counter offer after an employee gives notice... they also listen to see if an employee is vulnerable to a counter shortly after the move. If you believe an employee has severed all ties to their prior company... I will send you out for a drug test! Smart employers purposely stay in touch with former employees to listen for the signs of discontent and then capitalize on that discontent with an overture to that employee who may be having second thoughts about the move. I know I did as an HR director. I purposely had their friends from our company contact them to see how they were doing. If we sensed the person might be receptive to returning to our organization, we attacked that vulnerability like a battalion of tanks during the Battle of the Bulge in WWII. We had nothing to lose and everything to gain!

Orientation is not hard. Unfortunately, we see it as processing paperwork or an annoyance. I have several simple guidelines to make orientations SIMPLE and EFFECTIVE. All you have to do is:

▶ Have a formal process with the steps documented so you don't miss anything... a simple checklist is all you need.

▶ Have someone enthusiastic lead the orientation process.

▶ Break your orientation up over several days... or even weeks.

▶ NEVER ask the new employee to sit in a room filling out forms or going over policies for more than three hours.

▶ Include the immediate supervisor in the process. After all, the people won't be reporting to HR. Let the new person get to know their immediate supervisor right from the start.

▶ Expect the supervisor or manager to have a documented education training schedule for the new hire. The sink-or-swim method may work... but it also drowns a lot of good employees!

▶ Have senior level people introduce themselves during orientation and—ideally—have them present part of the orientation. It will wow the new employee to have someone in senior management actually take the time to play a role in the orientation process.

▶ Ensure that the tools they need to do the job are waiting for them on the first day: desk, computer, phone and basic office supplies.

- ► Assign a buddy to shadow this person for a period of time, someone who will spend time with the new hire. Pick an employee of yours who believes in the organization so you can build on the positive energy that the new employee brings to the job. The buddy should be someone who can show new hires how things *really get done* and where she can go for resources. Remember, if you don't select someone to shadow your new employee, the biggest complainer will do it, and will perform your orientation for you!

- ► Develop a list of FAQ's for new people, and include with it the names of the people in the company who are best equipped to handle key questions, along with their contact information.

- ► Introduce new employees to people. That's a simple courtesy. When guests show up at a party, you wouldn't greet them at the door, then say, "See ya' later!" Why? Because you want them to feel welcome. A new employee is no different.

- ► Never allow new employees to eat lunch alone for the first several weeks. It is critical that they become socialized into the organization and feel a part of their new home. Don't underestimate the retention power of social relationships. I worked at one organization where we took note of whether a new employee was eating lunch with someone at the end of the first week. If they were, it greatly increased the chances that they would stay with the organization. We instituted a buddy system and assigned someone to hang with each new hire to make him or her feel at home. And it worked. The buddy system also paid in dividends: if the newbie had concerns, we knew immediately and could address them.

▶ Check in with new employees at regular pre-set intervals. Ask them how they are doing. Listen to the responses and pick up on any signs that may indicate they are struggling... then act on the signals.

THESE GUIDELINES WORK! Just look at any branch of the U.S. military. The military does the best job of any organization I've seen in training and assimilating a diverse population into a cohesive group that will work together toward a common goal. If you have military veterans or former members of the military in your organization, tap into their expertise on this. They can tell you how the best do it! Use the elements above as a starting point, add your vets' expertise and build a dynamite orientation that will enhance your retention.

Get a group of managers together and brainstorm additional ways your company might kick-start the productivity of new employees while also driving retention. Then, start to rebuild your orientation.

▶ If you don't conduct orientation... your worst employee will do it for you.

▶ Orientation should include more than just filling out paperwork.

no
nonsense
notes

▶ Keep your orientation sessions under three hours. Hold more sessions if need be, but never exceed three hours for any single session.

▶ Pair your new employee with a buddy to guide them through the first few months.

14

Humor:
Lighten Up and
Have Some Fun!

WHY DO WE act as if having fun on the job is illegal? It's no wonder that employees struggle to get up in the morning and come in to work. We have moved from requiring suits to allowing business casual attire while, at the same time, becoming more uptight than we were 25 years ago when we wore ties. Ironically, people working in companies now appear unhappier than ever. It wasn't always that way. We wonder why people are miserable, why they're always wondering if there isn't a better place to work. I call it the Grass-is-Always-Greener Syndrome.

More intense competition and fear of getting close to our people has rendered most organizations humorless, particularly during downturns in the economy such as the recession we are experiencing as I write this book. The thinking seems to be that if you don't look serious, intense and austere, you can't be working very hard. Many organizations have adopted that philosophy. Why does it need to be? In my opinion, if you aren't enjoying your work, you're probably not attacking your work with an energy that customers can feel. You are not very engaged. You are putting in your time. As a company owner or manager, the last thing you want is employees who feel as if they are "doing time." You're not running a jail, you're running a company.

If, by some stroke of luck, you develop an environment where people laugh and have fun, the edge you will have over your competitors will be beyond imagination. Why? When your turnover drops, you will no longer be losing the knowledge that drives quality and productivity and this will give you a tremendous competitive advantage. Imagine working in HR and not continuously hiring new people. Or, when you do seek new employees, having the pick of the best people because everyone has heard about the quality of your work environment. That alone is reason enough to give it a try. But also think about the difference it would make if your people were looking forward to coming in every morning... because they enjoyed their work. Imagine what it would be like if people had fun. Just imagine the following benefits to your company.

- ▶ Lower absenteeism... they want to be there.
- ▶ More communication among people... they want to talk to each other.
- ▶ Excited, engaged employees speaking with your

customers... they want to talk to the customer... and the customer can feel it!

▶ An *esprit de corps* within your work group... they do not want to let their work group down.

The benefits of workers who enjoy their job are enormous. Part of the enjoyment grows out of the ability to have some fun on the job or, at the very least, to work in an environment that is not uptight. You will always have people who fight you on every little initiative. You know who they are. They're the ones who are never happy, who complain about everything, who are generally miserable and who don't look like they ever have any fun. What can you do to get the ball rolling and start to lighten up and have some fun?

RULE #1: Smile. Smiling goes a long way toward making *you* feel better and it sets an expectation that this is the norm for your people. Guess what? People will start to smile back. I used to joke with people who would never smiled by telling them they looked like their dog died. Then I'd jokingly tell them, "C'mon... smile." Guess what, they smiled. Smiling works.

RULE #2: Say good morning... even if it kills you! There will be *someone* who will not respond. Ah-ha! You have now found your future project. Seek that person out every morning and say, "Good morning," no matter what. Kill her with kindness. If you are a plant manager, general manager, vice president, owner, president or senior member of leadership, the first and second rules are essential. People will LOVE you and RESPECT you! Why? Because they are used to top management behaving like a bunch of suits, like stuffed shirts, like people totally lacking in humor. Smiling and saying "Good morning" does not diminish your professionalism, it enhances it. It makes you a "non-jerk." The number of senior leadership people I have seen walk by people in the hall without so much as a nod of the head, a smile, or any simple act of acknowledgement is countless. I can't print the adjectives people used to describe them. The result: No one respects them and certainly no one goes the extra mile for them. Bottom line: Not smiling is bad for the business!

RULE #3: Laugh. There is always something to laugh about. Find the humor in situations and laugh about them with your people. Before you know it, you will be laughing with your people and with fellow managers and situations that appeared negative will be seen in a different light. OMG... is that possible?

RULE #4: Don't take yourself so seriously. Seriously! Life is too short to view everything as life and death. We need to be serious about serving the customer... not serious for the purpose of being serious.

After you begin to apply these four basic rules, you can start to look at injecting some fun into your "sphere of influence." But... at a minimum... start to follow the four rules. That is the meat and potatoes. Anything beyond that is *pure gravy*.

If you want to take a peek at some of the gravy, get the book *Fish! Tales: Real-Life Stories to Help You Transform Your Workplace and Your Life*. I love *Fish! Tales*. If you have not read it, read it. You may not do some of the wild and crazy things featured in the book, but it may give you permission to lighten up a bit and do something fun. If you can increase retention in a call center, you can increase retention anywhere (*Fish! Tales*, ChartHouse Learning, 2002).

I am not one of those wild and crazy guys who does karaoke or likes to dress up in weird outfits. That's not me. (Although I have been known to wear a Hawaiian shirt!) I only wish I could be one of those people. The plus side is that I guarantee you have those type of people hiding somewhere in your environment. Let them start to be that person who is inside of them... as long as the customer is taken care of, the parts get out the door, and your quality is what it needs to be. *Your job: Create an atmosphere where people feel they can be themselves. Fun will follow. Better yet... tap into their ideas and start to try some of the fun things they think about.*

Think about a time at work where you had one of those embarrassing situations or when disaster occurred. Now... go talk to one of your co-workers who were there with you. I guarantee you will start laughing! The worst situations seem to be hilarious when we look back on them.

Make it a point to say "good morning" and smile when you greet every person in your department... every morning! Start tomorrow and keep a log to keep you on track.

Buy the book *Fish! Tales*. Read it. Now try to come up with your own type fun at work. Start to develop your "fun" style then ask some of your fun people for their ideas.

**no
nonsense
notes**

▶ Don't take yourself so seriously.

▶ Laugh.

▶ See the positives in every situation.

▶ Smile!

▶ Say "Good morning"... with a smile.

▶ Humor is *not* illegal in the workplace.

▶ Fun people are hidden in your organization... find them and tap into their expertise.

15
Conclusion

What's My Number... and How Do I Improve It?

BY NOW YOU should KNOW what your turn-over is. If you have been doing the **TIPS** you have already started to put together a comprehensive strategy to increase your retention. Now... consciously sit down with several of your fellow managers or your staff if you are in a senior executive and brainstorm other ideas based on the various sections of the book. This is where everyone starts to get nervous. You actually have to get off your duff and do something. That's why I wrote this book in the format I did. Hopefully, you will have been trying the **TIPS** all along and my request isn't like taking a leap off of a cliff without a safety harness. But... if you are feeling some nervousness... here is a story that may help you.

I was an HR director in a software development firm where turnover was a constant problem because of the nature of the business and other issues we were experiencing. Here's how I built our retention strategy. I sat down with managers, VP's, my boss, software developers... anyone who would sit down with me. We came up with ideas. I had this huge whiteboard that was 4' high by 15' long in my office. We put the ideas on the board. Everyone in the company could see them when they walked by my office... people stopped in and added to them... and then we started doing what we had on the board. Guess what? It worked. Not only did the ideas improve retention... we actually saw an improvement in other business metrics like customer service, productivity, and quality as well. My boss, the president, saw the results, and so did the managers who helped me with it. The corporation got what they wanted... higher profits... and we had a better place to work. That's the bottom line. And I started from scratch! You are half way there if you have been doing the **TIPS**. Just keep adding to them and your retention strategy will be formed.

Are you ready to take that leap? Will you live happily ever after? If you take that leap, the results will be both personally and professionally rewarding. I leave you with this quote as a final thought, to give you the courage to move forward.

∾

Far better is it to dare mighty things, to win glorious triumphs, even though checkered by failure... than to rank with those poor spirits who neither enjoy nor suffer much, because they live in a gray twilight that knows not victory nor defeat.

—Teddy Roosevelt

Bibliography

Buckingham, Marcus and Curt Coffman. *First, Break All the Rules: What the World's Best Managers Do Differently.* Simon & Schuster, New York, New York. 1999.

Certo, S.C. *Modern Management: Diversity, Quality, Ethics, and the Global Environment* (11th ed.). Allyn and Bacon, Upper Saddle River, New Jersey. 2009.

Christensen, John, Stephen Lundin, Harry Paul and Phillip Strand. *Fish! Tales: Real-Life Stories to Help You Transform Your Workplace and Your Life.* ChartHouse Learning, New York, New York. 2002.

Collins, Jim. *Good to Great: Why Some Companies Make the Leap ... and Others Don't.* HarperBusiness, New York, New York. 2001.

Gitomer, Jeffrey. *Little Gold Book of YES! Attitude: How to Find, Build and Keep a YES! Attitude for a Lifetime of SUCCESS.* FT Press, Upper Saddle River, New Jersey. 2006.

Sanborn, Mark. *The Fred Factor.* Doubleday Publishing Company, New York, New York. 2004.

Sibson Consulting: www.sibson.com/publications/surveysandstudies/2006 ROWno5.pdf

Thayer, Lee. *Leadership: Thinking, Being, Doing.* WME Books, Rochester, New York. 2007.

Visit **jeffkortes.com** to:

▶ Order the book *Employee Retention Fundamentals: No Nonsense Strategies to Retain Your Best People*

▶ Have Jeff speak about *Employee Retention Fundamentals* to your oganization or team

▶ Sign up to get weekly *Employee Retention Fundamentals* videos

Or call or e-mail:

414-421-9626
jeff@humanassetmgt.com

Bring out the best in your organization

If you are interested in employee retention programs based on the *Employee Retention Fundamentals* principles, contact Human Asset Management, LLC at:

Phone: **414-421-9626**
E-mail: **jeff@humanassetmgt.com**

To purchase bulk copies of *Employee Retention Fundamentals* for large groups or your organization at a discount, please contact us at the phone number or e-mail address above.